DATE DUE

21st Century Skills INNOVATION LIBRARY

MAKERS
As Innovators

Web Design with HTML5

CHERRY LAKE PUBLISHING • ANN ARBOR, MICHIGAN

by Colleen van Lent

CHERRY LAKE
Publishing

A Note to Adults: Please review the instructions for the activities in this book before allowing children to do them. Be sure to help them with any activities you do not think they can safely complete on their own.

A Note to Kids: Be sure to ask an adult for help with these activities when you need it. Always put your safety first!

Published in the United States of America by Cherry Lake Publishing
Ann Arbor, Michigan
www.cherrylakepublishing.com

Series editor: Kristin Fontichiaro

Photo Credits: Cover and page 1, The Design Lab; pages 7, 12, and 21, Colleen van Lent; pages 27 and 29, Courtesy of Michigan Makers.

Library of Congress Cataloging-in-Publication Data
Van Lent, Colleen.
  Web Design with HTML5 / by Colleen Van Lent.
    pages cm. — (Makers as innovators)
  Includes bibliographical references and index.
  ISBN 978-1-63137-773-0 (lib. bdg.) — ISBN 978-1-63137-793-8 (pbk.) — ISBN 978-1-63137-833-1 (e-book) — ISBN 978-1-63137-813-3 (pdf)
  1. HTML (Document markup language)—Juvenile literature. 2. Internet programming—Juvenile literature. 3. Web sites—Juvenile literature. I. Title.
  QA76.76.H94V36 2015
  006.7'4—dc23   2014009253

Cherry Lake Publishing would like to acknowledge the work of The Partnership for 21st Century Skills. Please visit www.p21.org for more information.

Printed in the United States of America
Corporate Graphics Inc.
July 2014

Contents

Chapter 1

What Is HTML?

Using the Internet is easier now than it has ever been. Almost everyone uses it to look at their favorite sites, and even beginners can easily post content such as photos, videos, and **blog** entries. Not everyone knows how to build a Web page from scratch, though. If you want to know about the nuts and bolts that make the Web work, you will need to learn hypertext markup language (HTML). HTML is a set of codes and commands that can be used to build Web pages.

A computer is a powerful device. However, it needs clear instructions from a user to work properly. You need to tell the computer exactly what you want it to do and how you want it to be done. Web designers use HTML to "mark up" content (such as words, images, and videos) with **tags**. The tags tell computers how to display content on a screen and how users can interact with it.

Tags are simple code words or abbreviations that are placed inside the symbols < and >. People cannot see the tags when they use a **browser** to visit a Web page. Instead, the tags work behind the scenes.

For example, if you have a Web page, you might want to make some words appear in bold text. To do this, you would need two tags. The first one is <b>. This is called an opening tag. It goes at the beginning of the words you want to make bold. The second one is </b>. This is called a closing tag. It goes at the end of the words you want to make bold. Any words you type between these two tags will show up in bold text in a Web browser. (So don't forget to use end tags!)

In other words, if you want to make text bold, place it between tags <b> and </b>. If you type,

```
<b>This text is bold</b>
```

a Web browser will display it as

This text is bold.

Plan Before You Code!

Before you dive in to learn more HTML tags, you might want to think about the type of Web page you want to make. When you write an essay, you probably start by making an outline. Similarly, the first step in making a Web page is to sketch your ideas out on paper. There are a lot of decisions to make before you start typing out your code. What do you want to say (words) or show (pictures or links)? Do you want to use paragraphs or lists to organize your information? Will you organize the page into sections? Will each section have its own **heading**? What will the page's **layout** look like? What color should the background be?

Let's look at a sample page on page 7 of this book. You can also view this sample page online at http://cherrylakepublishing.com/activities. It has three sections:

Tons of Tags

Tags are the commands designers use to mark up the text in an HTML document. In this book, you'll learn the most commonly used tags. However, there are many others you can use to give your Web pages a more interesting look or add new features. Try searching online to learn about the huge variety of HTML tags you can use. For example, try visiting www.w3.org/TR/html-markup/elements.html.

HTML was first introduced in the early 1990s. Since then, it has been improved with new versions. The Internet is always changing, and Web developers continue to add new tags to keep up with new technology. The most recent version of HTML is called HTML5. You won't need to start from scratch when HTML6 eventually comes out, though. Each new version simply adds tags to the old ones.

page with blue
background

tab title

header with white
background

image →

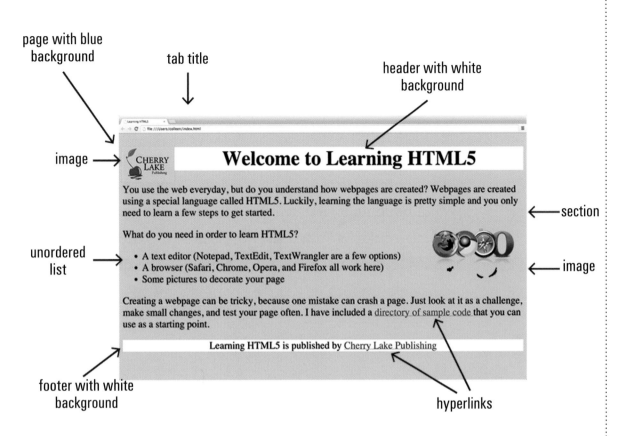

section

unordered
list

image

footer with white
background

hyperlinks

- The top section, or header, has the name of the
  page (Welcome to Learning HTML5) and a
  picture (the Cherry Lake Publishing logo).
- The middle section has the main content. In this
  example, it includes a few paragraphs of text, a
  list, a link, and another image.
- The bottom section, or footer, has information
  about who owns the page and another link.

Now that you know the basic parts that make up a
Web page, let's learn how to put them together!

Chapter 2

Getting Started

Once you have a general idea of your Web page's layout and content, you can start coding. Even if you are new to coding, it isn't very difficult to get started. The key is to work carefully, save often, and test your page in a browser frequently. There are three main steps.

1. Create an HTML file.
2. Add the three main components (doctype, head, and body) of a Web page.
3. View your page and revise it as needed. Repeat this step until you are done.

You can use a simple text editing program to create HTML files. Most computers come with at least one of these programs installed. On Windows computers, you can use Notepad. On Macs, you can use TextEdit. There are also text editing programs available for tablet computers, but it is much easier to use a desktop or laptop computer when creating Web pages.

Have you ever noticed that when you double-click on a file, it opens automatically using the correct program? The computer examines the file extension to know which program it should use to open the file. File extensions are the three- or four-letter codes that follow a file name. For example, Microsoft Word documents use .doc or .docx. An image might use .jpg or .gif. Web pages usually use .html as the file extension. This extension tells your computer to open the file using a Web browser such as Internet Explorer, Safari, Chrome, or Firefox.

If you find that your browser can't open the Web page you made, it might be because you forgot to put ".html" at the end of the file name. Open your file again in your text editor and click on File, Save As, so you can add .html to the end of the file name.

Adding the Three Main Components

To begin, open a new file in your text editing program and save it as index.html. Each Web document is made up of three parts:

Doctype

The doctype tells browsers which version of HTML is being used. The doctype for HTML5 is simply:

```
<!DOCTYPE html>
```

Head

The head contains **metadata**. Metadata provides additional information to the browser but is not displayed to the user. For now, the only thing you will add to the head is the title of your Web page.

Body

The body is the part of the page that people actually see in their browsers. It can contain anything you want!

You will need to use tags to indicate where each of the three sections begins and ends. Type the code below into your index.html document. Make sure that each opening tag (except for the !DOCTYPE) has a closing tag!

```html
<!DOCTYPE html>
<html>
   <head>
   </head>

   <body>
   </body>
</html>
```

As you work, keep your HTML file open in a browser and text editor at the same time. Whenever you change the code in the text editor, save the file. Then reload the page in your browser to see how your changes have affected the page. This will allow you to check your work as you go.

Adding Content

What do you see when you view the code from the previous page in a browser? If you did it right, you won't see anything at all! The only things in your HTML file are tags. There is no content! Go back to the text editor and add some text between the tags:

```
<!DOCTYPE html>
<html>
   <head>
   </head>

   <body>
     My name is Colleen. This is my first Web page.
   </body>
</html>
```

The resulting Web page should look something like this:

Next, add a title to your Web page. The title will show up at the top of the browser tab or window. Right now, the title is index.html, your file name. Make it something descriptive instead.

```
<!DOCTYPE html>
<html>
  <head>
    <title> My First Page </title>
  </head>

  <body>
    My name is Colleen. This is my first Web page.

  </body>
</html>
```

Let's jazz up the page and make it look better. Remember, browsers need a lot of instructions. If you type spaces, tabs, and blank lines into your html file, browsers will ignore them. Do you see the extra spaces in the code below? When the browser displays this file, the spaces will disappear, and the page will look just like it did in the previous example.

```
<!DOCTYPE html>
<html>
 <head>
 <title> My First Page </title>
 </head>

 <body>
 My     name is     Colleen. This
 is my     first

   Web page.

 </body>
</html>
```

The only way to format text in HTML is with tags. Let's learn how to use some of the most common ones!

Chapter 3

Common Tags

In the past, Internet connections were not as fast as they are today. Web designers tried to avoid adding too many photos or design elements that would make their pages load too slowly. With today's speedy Internet connections, designers don't have to worry so much about how quickly their pages load. They are free to be as creative as possible when designing the way their pages look. Tags make it possible to perk up your page's appearance.

Let's start with the top and bottom of your page. The top section is called the header. It is marked by the tag <header>. The bottom is called the footer. It is marked by the tag <footer>. Headers usually contain important introductory information such as the title or author. The footer often contains **copyright** and contact information.

Block Tags

Some tags apply to a whole chunk of text, like footers, headers, paragraphs, and lists. These are called block tags. A browser adds a line break before and after these tags. Let's look at some common block tags.

Paragraphs: <p>

You will use paragraph tags each time you start or end a paragraph. Remember, your browser will ignore blank lines between paragraphs in your HTML code. You must use the paragraph tag instead.

Headings: <h1> through <h6>

There are six codes for headings: <h1>, <h2>, <h3>, <h4>, <h5>, and <h6>. The *smaller* the heading's number, the *larger* the font size will be for the text that follows.

Lists: <ol>, <ul>, and <li>

It takes two sets of tags to create a list. The first tag is <ol> or <ul>. These stand for "ordered list" (numbered) and "unordered list" (decorative or bulleted). They tell the computer, "Let's start making a list!" You also need to tell the computer what items are in the list. Put <li> (for "list item") before and </li> after each item so the computer knows where to start and stop a new item in the list.

It is a pretty common mistake to forget the closing tags </ol>, </ul>, and </li>. If you don't include these tags, a browser will keep displaying the rest of your page as a list!

```
<ol>
    <li> Apples </li>
    <li> Bananas </li>
</ol>
```

```
<ul>
    <li> Apples </li>
    <li> Bananas </li>
</ul>
```

```
1. Apples
2. Bananas
```

```
• Apples
• Bananas
```

Inline Elements

Inline elements can make individual words or phrases look or work differently. They appear next to other other elements, rather than above or below like block elements. Let's look at some common ones:

Hyperlinks: <a href = " ">

Whenever you click on text, images, or other elements and get sent to a different Web page, you're using hyperlinks. Links are important because they let you connect Web pages and other content together. You can link to your own creations or send people to any other site on the Web.

You need the tag <a> to insert links into a page. You also need some helper tools called attributes. Attributes are located inside a tag's brackets. They provide additional information for the tag, such as the address of the page you want to link to. The attribute for a hyperlink is "href=" followed by the location of the content you are linking to.

If the code looks like this ...	It will do this ...
<a href = "http://www.google.com">	Link to the Google home page
<a href = "page2.html">	Link to a file named page2.html
<a href = "imgs/mypic.jpg">	Link to an image file named mypic.jpg that is in a folder named imgs

After opening the <a> tag and adding a link attribute, we still need to indicate which part of the Web page will turn into a clickable link. Let's say we want to link to the University of Michigan home page. The site's Web address, or URL, is www.umich.edu. Include that URL inside the opening tag, after "href=". After the entire opening tag, type "University of Michigan." Then enter the closing tag, which is just </a>.

It should look like this in your text editor:

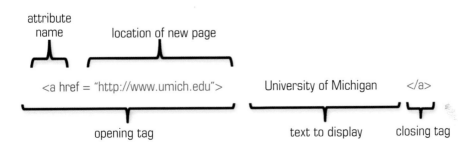

In a browser, it should show up like this:

<u>University of Michigan</u>

If you click on the underlined words "University of Michigan," your browser will take you to www.umich.edu. Cool! You've just joined the World Wide Web! It is easy to make mistakes when you're learning how to make links, so go slowly and check your work. Before you know it, you'll have it down!

Images: <img/>

Images make your Web page look great! Take a look at the code on the facing page. Do you notice anything interesting about the tag? It doesn't have separate opening and closing pieces! This is known as a self-closing tag. To put an image on your page, you only need this one tag. However, you need to include two attributes.

First, you need to enter the location of the image you want displayed, using the code "src". You also need to fill in the "alt" attribute. This attribute provides the browser with words to describe the image. These words are displayed if the browser can't find the image or if the person visiting the page is using a device to read Web pages aloud. This is especially important for any blind people who visit your page. The alt text will help them understand what is on the screen. The following code instructs a browser to show a picture of a dog and provides alt text.

```
<img src="Rover.jpg"    alt="My dog Rover"/>
```

Your image source can be a picture that is on your computer (and later published online along with your Web page—see chapter 5). It can also be a link to a picture that is already on the Internet. If you want to use a picture you find on the Web, you need to include its full URL (for example, http://www.othersite.com/picture.jpg). You can usually find an image's URL by right-clicking on the picture and selecting the Copy Image URL option. Make sure you get permission before posting on your Web page images that belong to other people.

You can also add your own images to a Web page. If you upload your own pictures, your image attribute can just include the file name (for example: picture.jpg, photo.gif, Rover.png) instead of the whole URL.

These tags will allow you to create most of the sample page from chapter 1. Download the images from http://cherrylakepublishing.com/activities. Then use the code below to help get you started.

```html
<!DOCTYPE html>
<html>
<head>
  <title>Learning HTML5</title>
</head>

<body>
  <header>
    <img src ="CherryLake.png" alt = "CherryLake Logo"; />
    <h1>Welcome to Learning HTML5</h1>
  </header>

  <section>

    <p>You use the web every day, but do you understand how Web pages are created?
    Web pages are created using a special language called HTML5. Luckily, learning the
    language is pretty simple and you only need to learn a few steps to get started.</p>

    <p>What do you need in order to learn HTML5?
      <img src = "http://upload.wikimedia.org/wikipedia/commons/7/78/MultiBrowsers.png"
      alt = "Internet browsers"/></p>
    <ul>
    <li>A text editor (Notepad, TextEdit, TextWrangler are a few options)</li>
    <li>A browser (Safari, Chrome, Opera, and Firefox all work here)</li>
    <li>Some pictures to decorate your page</li>
    </ul>
      <p>Creating a Web page can be tricky, because one mistake can crash a page.
          Just look at it as a challenge, make small changes, and test your page often.
          I have included a <a href = "Samples">directory of sample code </a> that you
          can use as a starting point.</p>

    </section>
    <footer>
    Learning HTML5 is published by <a href = "http://cherrylakepublishing com/">
    Cherry Lake Publishing</a>
</footer>
</body>
</html>
```

Feel free to change or modify the code to make it your own! Make sure that you place your image files in the same folder as your html file.

If you used the images from http://cherrylake publishing.com/activities, your page should look something like this:

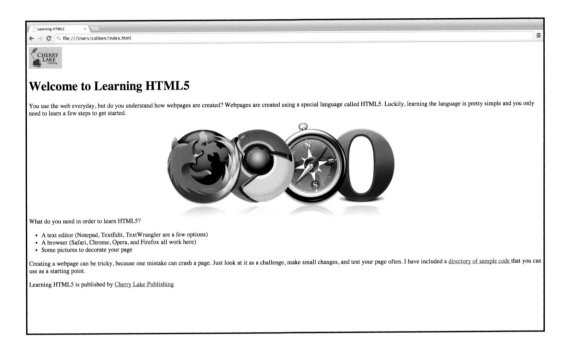

The content is all there, but the appearance isn't quite the same as the sample page from chapter 1. Where are the colors? Turn to the next chapter to find out!

Tremendous Tags

Here is a handy reference for the tags you learned about in this chapter. These tags will be a big part of your Web design projects, from the simplest pages to the most complex sites.

Common Block Tags

Block tags apply to an entire chunk of a Web page.

- **<header>** identifies the very top of the page
- **<footer>** identifies the very bottom of the page
- **<p>** marks the start of a paragraph
- **<h1> through <h6>** identify headings
- **<ol>** begins an ordered, or numbered, list
- **<ul>** begins an unordered list, such as a list of bullet points
- **<li>** marks a new item in a list

Common Inline Tags

Inline tags can happen in the middle of a line, paragraph, or sentence.

- **<a>** creates a hyperlink to a different Web page or other content
- **<img/>** displays an image

Common Attributes

These codes appear inside tags and help tags do their job.

- **href** points a hyperlink toward the URL of a Web page or some other content
- **src** indicates the location of an image or other content
- **alt** displays words to describe images
- **style** changes the look of text or other elements on the page

Chapter 4

Formatting Your Page

All of your tags are in place, but your page doesn't look quite like you wanted it to. It is time to add some style attributes to the tags. In this chapter, we'll change our page's background color and learn how to line up text along the left, center, or right side of a browser window.

Background Colors: style=" :"
In order to add a background color to the different sections, you need to modify the tags to include a style attribute. Let's start with the body of the page.

```
<body style="background: RoyalBlue;">
```

This tells the browser that the page should have a bright blue background. Let's set a separate color for the header and footer.

```
<header style="background:white;">
```

```
<footer style="background:white;">
```

Keep an eye on the punctuation needed for each tag and attribute. Add this code and save your file. Check your page in a browser to make sure the color has been added. If it didn't change, reload your page again and make sure you are looking at the most recent version of the HTML file. It seems like a silly mistake to test the wrong page, but it happens all the time!

Positioning Text: text-align

As you now know, the footer is a place where many Web designers remind visitors who owns the work. Let's say we want to add this copyright information to the bottom of our page:

Copyright 2015 by Jose

The text above is centered on the screen. We can use attributes to tell the browser to align different chunks of text (such as h1 tags) along the left, center, or right of the browser window. See the codes on page 27.

Avoid including your last name in the copyright information on your pages. It is very important to keep that kind of personal information off of the Internet. See chapter 5 for more on Internet safety.

We want to do three things: add copyright text to the footer, center it, and make its background white. Here's what the code for that looks like in HTML5:

```
<footer style = "background: white; text-align: center">
```

Positioning Images: float

Sometimes you want your images to appear next to text instead of under or over it. The float attribute can do this for you. The code to place the logo to the left of the text is:

```
<img src="CherryLake.png"    alt="CherryLake Logo"  style = "float: left; />
```

Sometimes a picture is too big. You can use the width attribute to resize it to look better. Add the code:

```
width = "25%"    style = "float: right;"
```

to the image tag and the browser picture will size nicely and to the right.

Now that you've added background colors, text alignment (also known as justification), and image formatting your complete code should look like the code below, and your Web page should look like the one in chapter 1!

Review your code carefully to check for mistakes.

```
<!DOCTYPE html>
<html>
<head>
  <title>Learning HTML5</title>
</head>

<body style = "background: RoyalBlue;">
  <header style = "background:white;">
<img src = "CherryLake.png" alt = "CherryLake Logo" style = "float: left;"/>
    <h1 style = "text-align: center;">Welcome to Learning HTML5</h1>
  </header>

  <section>

<p>You use the Web everyday, but do you understand how Web pages are created?
Web pages are created using a special language called HTML5. Luckily, learning the
language is pretty simple and you only need to learn a few steps to get started.</p>
<p>What do you need in order to learn HTML5?
    <img src="http://upload.wikimedia.org/wikipedia/commons/7/78/MultiBrowsers.png"
        alt = "Internet browsers" width = "25%" style="float:right;"/></p>
<ul>
<li>A text editor (Notepad, TextEdit, TextWrangler are a few options)</li>
<li>A browser (Safari, Chrome, Opera, and Firefox all work here)</li>
<li>Some pictures to decorate your page</li>
</ul>
<p>Creating a Web page can be tricky, because one mistake can crash a page.
Just look at it as a challenge, make small changes, and test your page often.
I have included a <a href = "Samples"> directory of sample code </a> that you
can use as a starting point.</p>
  </section>

  <footer style = "background:white; text-align: center;">
  Learning HTML5 is published by <a href = "http://cherrylakepublishing.com">
  Cherry Lake Publishing</a>
</footer>
</body>
</html>
```

There are certain color names that are automatically recognized by most Web browsers. Here is a brief list:

- white
- black
- greenyellow
- lightpink
- firebrick
- dodgerblue
- purple
- slategray

Most Web designers like having a wider variety of colors. They avoid using color names and instead identify colors by a hashtag (#) plus a special six-digit code known as a hexadecimal value.

You can find a complete list of Web colors with their names and codes at www.webdevelopersnotes.com/design/list_of_HTML_color_names.php3

Alignmnet

Unless you tell a browser otherwise, it will assume that you want all of your text to start on the left side of the page. This is called left justification or left alignment. If you want to have text line up on the right side or be centered (or switch back to left justification when you're done), you need to use the text-align attribute:

- text-align: left
- text-align: center
- text-align: right

Chapter 5

Publishing and Beyond

Congratulations on finishing your first Web page! Right now, the only way to see it is to look at your computer. If you want other people to see it, you will need to publish it to the Internet. This will require two things. First, you will need a **domain name**, such as myawesomepage.com. You will also need **server** space to store your Web site's files online. You can purchase both of these things online, but check with your school or parents first. You might even be able to find a server that will host your site for free!

Internet Safety

It is important to keep privacy and safety in mind anytime you post information on the Internet. Get your parents' permission before publishing a Web page online. Never include personal information on your Web page. This includes your full name, home address, school, e-mail address, and phone number. Be selective about the pictures you post, too. You never know who will be looking at your page. Strangers could use your personal information to hurt or bother you. In addition, posting your e-mail address online could result in a bunch of junk mail showing up in your inbox!

You've learned some common HTML tags and attributes, but there's so much more you can do with Web pages! Try looking at the HTML code for Web pages you visit online. Most browsers will give you the option to "View Source" if you right-click anywhere on a Web page. When you do, a new window or tab will display the page's HTML code. Try copying the code into your own HTML files and experimenting with it to see how different tags work. This is a great way to learn new Web design tricks.

With a little practice, you can become an author—not just a viewer—of the Web. Whether you want to write a blog about your favorite TV show or create a Web page for a school project, your HTML skills will come in handy. You can be in charge of your corner of the Web. <b> Good luck! </b>

Glossary

blog (BLAHG) a Web page or Web site to which new messages are added easily

browser (BROU-zur) a computer program that lets you find and look through Web pages or other data

copyright (KAH-pee-rite) the legal right to control the use of something created, such as a song or book

domain name (doh-MAYN NAYM) a general address on the World Wide Web

heading (HED-ing) words written as a title at the top of a page or over a section of writing

layout (LAY-owt) the way text, images, and other elements are arranged on a Web page

metadata (MEH-tuh-da-tuh) HTML code that includes information about a Web page but is not visible when viewing the page in a browser

server (SUR-vur) a computer shared by two or more users in a network

tags (TAGZ) codes that tell a computer how it should deal with text or data

Find Out More

BOOKS

Martin, Chris. *Build Your Own Web Site*. New York:
Rosen Central, 2014.

Poolos, Jamie. *Designing, Building, and Maintaining Web Sites*.
New York: Rosen Central, 2011.

WEB SITES

Codeacademy
www.codeacademy.com
Follow self-paced tutorials for learning HTML and other
programming languages.

Mozilla Webmaker
https://webmaker.org
Mozilla, the nonprofit organization behind the Firefox browser,
will teach you strategies for viewing source code and coding
your own pages.

Index

About the Author

Colleen van Lent is a computer scientist who teaches at the University of Michigan School of Information in Ann Arbor.